THIS JOURNEY BELONGS TO

....

For Sue & Colin

(and Ground Crews everywhere)

perfectly MUDDLED PUBLISHING
First published in the UK in 2024

ISBN: 978-1-7385514-0-8

My perfectly MUDDLED Journey to Space

S + G CARPENTER-DAY

A YOUNG, TRAINEE ASTRONAUT
WISHED ONE DAY SOON,
THAT THEY'D FLY INTO SPACE
AND TOUCH DOWN ON THE MOON.

BUT DREAMS CAN BE TRICKY
AND HARD TO ACHIEVE,
AND DEPEND ON THE JOURNEY
AND HELP YOU RECEIVE.

SAM'S JOURNEY BEGAN
AT A 'TOP SECRET' PLACE,
WHERE THEY TRAINED TO GET READY
TO FLY INTO SPACE.

SAM'S GROUND CREW WERE AWESOME
(AND KNEW SAM QUITE WELL).
THEY WERE THERE IN TOUGH TIMES
AND TO HELP IF SAM FELL.

THEY'D ANSWER SPACE QUESTIONS
(THEIR KNOWLEDGE WAS WEALTHY),
AND THEY'D FIND WAYS TO MAKE SURE
THAT SAM COULD STAY HEALTHY.

THEY GAVE SAM THE CHANCE
TO DREAM BIG AND AIM HIGH,
AND ENCOURAGED THEIR FRIEND
TO GIVE NEW THINGS A TRY.

CHOOSE KINDNESS
I Believe in You
Keep Going
GOOD JOB
SUPERB WORK
WONDERFUL EFFORT
YOU ROCK!
WAY TO GO

THEIR CARING AND KINDNESS
ALLOWED SAM TO GROW,
AND PREPARE FOR THE DAY
WHEN THE SPACE TEAM WOULD SHOW.

AND ALTHOUGH THEY WEREN'T SURE
IF THAT DAY WOULD BE SOON,
THEY GAVE IT THEIR ALL
TO GET SET FOR THE MOON...

AS WEEKS TURNED TO MONTHS,
SAM GREW AND GOT STRONG.
BUT WHEN WOULD THE SPACE TEAM
BE COMING ALONG?

THEN ONE DAY A LETTER ARRIVED FROM HQ:

THE GROUND CREW COULD SEE
SAM HAD DEEP, MIXED EMOTIONS.
FOR ALTHOUGH THEY'D BEEN TRAINING
TO FLY OVER OCEANS,

THE SPACE CADET RIGHTFULLY
HAD LOTS OF QUESTIONS,
SO THEY ASKED THEIR GROUND CREW
FOR THEIR THOUGHTS AND SUGGESTIONS.

WON'T IT BE SCARY
UP THERE, OUT IN SPACE?
I KNOW THAT I'LL MISS
YOUR WARM SMILE AND KIND FACE.

I DON'T KNOW THIS NEW TEAM
(ALTHOUGH THEY SOUND NICE),
SO BEFORE I HEAD OFF
I WOULD LOVE SOME ADVICE.

THE GROUND CREW WERE READY
(SOME HAD DONE THIS BEFORE),
AND THEY SHARED SOME KIND WORDS
THAT WOULD HELP SAM TO SOAR:

"WE ALL FEEL SO PROUD,
AS OUR MISSION IS DONE.
WE'VE ENJOYED ALL THE TRAINING,
HARD WORK, AND THE FUN...

IT'S BEEN QUITE AN HONOUR
TO BE AT YOUR SERVICE,
BUT NOW THE TIME'S COME
TO FULFIL YOUR LIFE'S PURPOSE.

WE'LL MISS YOU OF COURSE,
AND GOODBYES ARE A DEVIL,
BUT THE SPACE TEAM CAN HELP YOU
TO REACH THE NEXT LEVEL."

SPACE TRAINING STATION
NOW READY FOR BOARDING
YOU ARE awesome

AND SO THE DAY CAME
WHEN THE SPACE TEAM ARRIVED.
THE GROUND CREW GOT HUGS
AND THEY SAID THEIR GOODBYES.

THEN THE SPACE CADET LEFT
(STILL A LITTLE UNSURE),
BUT SAM KNEW THAT THE SPACE TEAM
WERE SAFE AND SECURE.

HEADQUARTERS LOOKED 'DIFFERENT'
(NEW SOUNDS & SMELLS TOO),
BUT IT SLOWLY BECAME SOMEWHERE
SAM FELT THEY KNEW.

THE NEW TEAM WERE PATIENT,
PLUS LOVELY AND KIND,
AND THEY LISTENED TO STORIES
OF THOSE LEFT BEHIND.

EACH TIME THAT THEY HELPED SAM
ACHIEVE A NEW DREAM,
SAM FELT THE BOND STRENGTHEN
AND GROW WITH THEIR TEAM!

WHEN ASKED IF THEY'D QUIT
THEY ASSURED SAM THEY WOULDN'T,
AND THEY HELPED SAM IN WAYS
THAT THE GROUND CREW JUST COULDN'T.

YES, ALL THOSE INVOLVED
FROM THE START TO THE END,
WANTED ONLY THE BEST
FOR THEIR ASTRONAUT FRIEND.

SAM MADE IT TO SPACE,
WITH THE TEAM WHO WERE NEW,
AND SAM ALWAYS REMEMBERED
THEIR FIRST TRAINING CREW.

Printed in Great Britain
by Amazon

57046705R00018